**IF FOUND, PLEASE RETURN TO:**

NAME _____

ADDRESS _____

_____

PHONE _____

E-MAIL _____

_____

ISBN 978-1-4521-8455-5

Manufactured in China.
Designed by Kayla Ferriera.

See the complete *One Sketch a Day* series
at www.chroniclebooks.com

10 9 8 7 6 5 4 3 2

Chronicle Books LLC
680 Second Street
San Francisco, CA 94107
www.chroniclebooks.com

# ONE SKETCH A DAY

## A VISUAL JOURNAL

CHRONICLE BOOKS

SAN FRANCISCO

# A YEARLONG RECORD OF SKETCHES–

because every daily drawing is
worthy of remembrance.

## HOW TO USE THIS SKETCHBOOK

Each page has space for two days of sketching. To begin, enter today's
and tomorrow's dates at the top and bottom entry of the first page.
Now just sharpen your pencil or take out your pen and let the creative
juices flow. You might find inspiration in your everyday surroundings,
or you can let your imagination run wild! However you fill these pages,
they will become a document of your creative journey over a year.

DAY 1                                     DATE   /  /

DAY 2                                     DATE   /  /

DAY 3                                          DATE    /    /

DAY 4                                          DATE    /    /

DAY 5                                                    DATE    /    /

DAY 6                                                    DATE    /    /

DAY 7                                    DATE    /    /

DAY 8                                    DATE    /    /

DAY 9                                          DATE    /    /

DAY 10                                         DATE    /    /

DAY 15                                                    DATE    /    /

DAY 16                                                    DATE    /    /

DAY 21                                    DATE    /    /

DAY 22                                    DATE    /    /

DAY 31                                          DATE    /    /

DAY 32                                          DATE    /    /

DAY 37                                          DATE    /    /

DAY 38                                          DATE    /    /

DAY 47                                          DATE    /    /

DAY 48                                          DATE    /    /

DAY 50

DAY 53                                    DATE    /    /

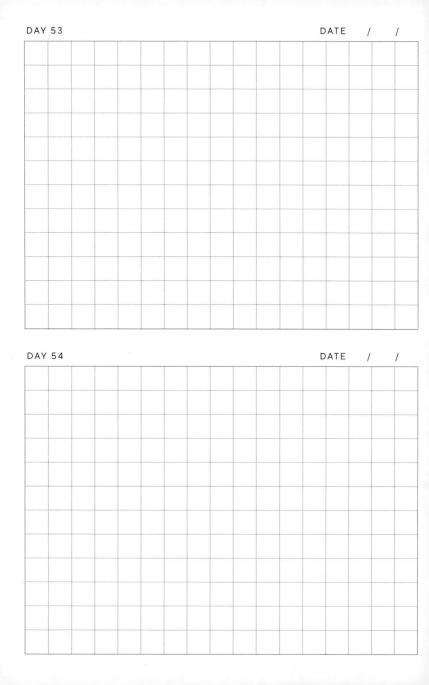

DAY 54                                    DATE    /    /

DAY 63 DATE / /

DAY 64 DATE / /

DAY 69                                    DATE    /    /

DAY 70                                    DATE    /    /

DAY 79                                    DATE    /    /

DAY 80                                    DATE    /    /

DAY 87                                    DATE    /    /

DAY 88                                    DATE    /    /

DAY 95                                        DATE    /    /

DAY 96                                        DATE    /    /

DAY 101 DATE / /

DAY 102 DATE / /

DAY 143                                          DATE    /    /

DAY 144                                          DATE    /    /

DAY 149                                    DATE    /    /

DAY 150                                    DATE    /    /

DAY 175                                           DATE    /    /

DAY 176                                           DATE    /    /

DAY 181                                          DATE   /   /

DAY 182                                          DATE   /   /

DAY 191    DATE   /   /

DAY 192    DATE   /   /

DAY 197                                           DATE    /    /

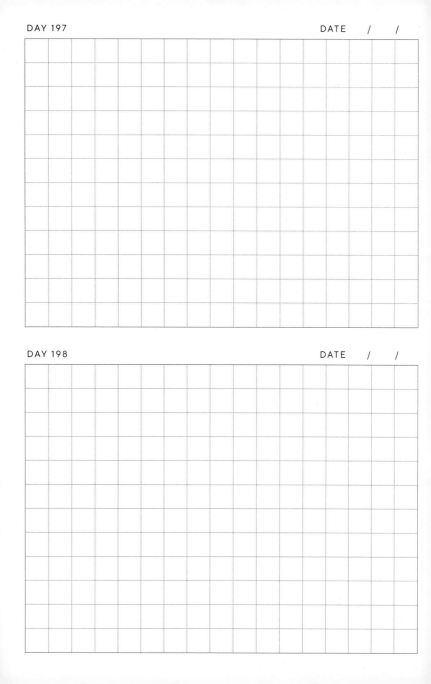

DAY 198                                           DATE    /    /

DAY 207                                                DATE    /    /

DAY 208                                                DATE    /    /

DAY 213                                    DATE    /    /

DAY 214                                    DATE    /    /

DAY 217                                    DATE    /    /

DAY 218                                    DATE    /    /

DAY 223                                          DATE    /    /

DAY 224                                          DATE    /    /

DAY 239     DATE    /    /

DAY 240     DATE    /    /

DAY 243                                    DATE    /    /

DAY 244                                    DATE    /    /

DAY 255                                           DATE    /    /

DAY 256                                           DATE    /    /

DAY 261　　　　　　　　　　　　　　　　　　　DATE　　/　　/

DAY 262　　　　　　　　　　　　　　　　　　　DATE　　/　　/

DAY 287          DATE   /   /

DAY 288          DATE   /   /

DAY 293                                          DATE    /    /

DAY 294                                          DATE    /    /

DAY 303                                        DATE    /    /

DAY 304                                        DATE    /    /

DAY 319                                    DATE    /    /

DAY 320                                    DATE    /    /

DAY 325                                    DATE    /    /

DAY 326                                    DATE    /    /

DAY 335                                          DATE    /    /

DAY 336                                          DATE    /    /

DAY 357					DATE    /    /

DAY 358					DATE    /    /

DATE / /

DATE / /

CONGRATULATIONS!

# YOU MADE ONE SKETCH A DAY FOR A YEAR.

**WHAT WILL YOU DO NEXT?**

# THINGS TO SKETCH

# FACES TO REMEMBER